I0461923

Sacred Sloths

COLORING BOOK

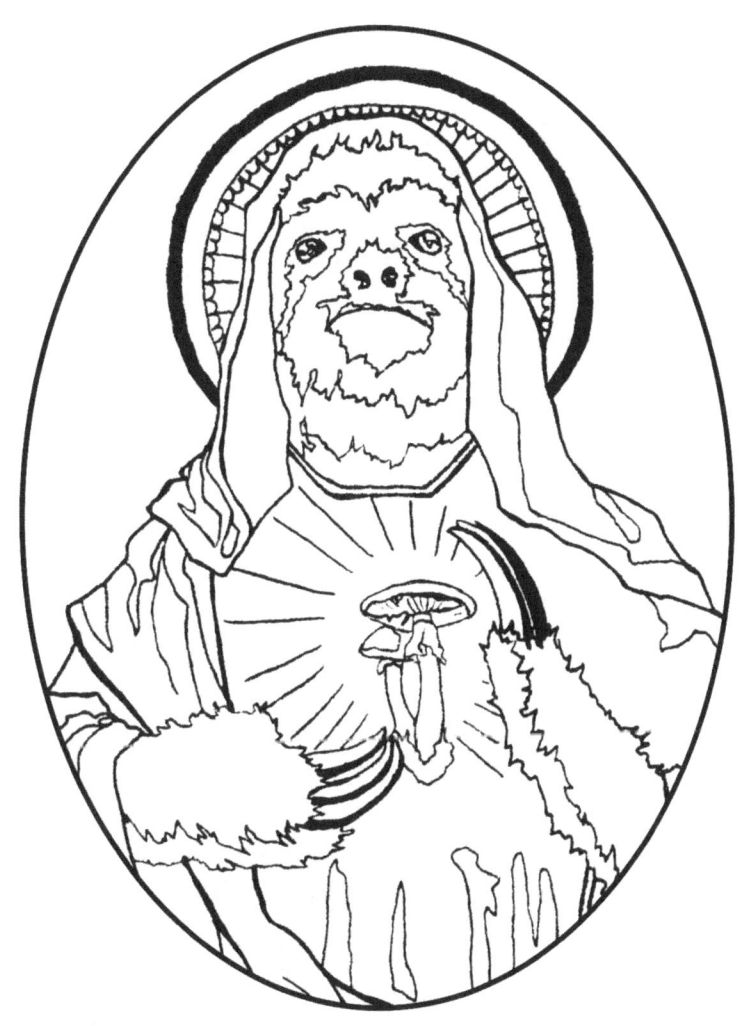

TWENTY SLOTHS TO COLOR ANY WAY YOU LIKE

WWW.ALISONDNEVILLE.COM

ILLUSTRATED BY
ALISON NEVILLE©2018

TWENTY DIFFERENT RELIGIONS HAVE BEEN SHOWN HERE WITH ONE OF MY FAVORITE ANIMALS: THE SLOTH. TRY TO GUESS THEM ALL AND SEE THE LAST PAGE FOR DETAILS. THERE IS ALSO A HIDDEN MUSHROOM IN EACH ILLUSTRATION TO PAY HOMAGE TO MY FIRST BOOK CALLED FUNGI FANCY.

OTHER TITLES INCLUDE: FUNGI FANCY AND SULTRY SEA SLUGS

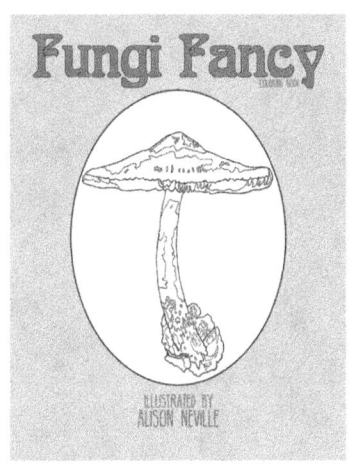
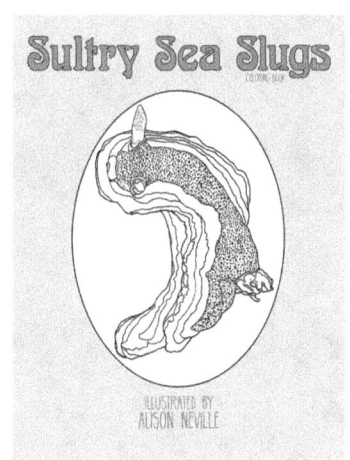

PUBLISHED 11/16/2018 BY

©ALISON NEVILLE

ISBN-13: 978-0578420080

ISBN-10: 0578420082

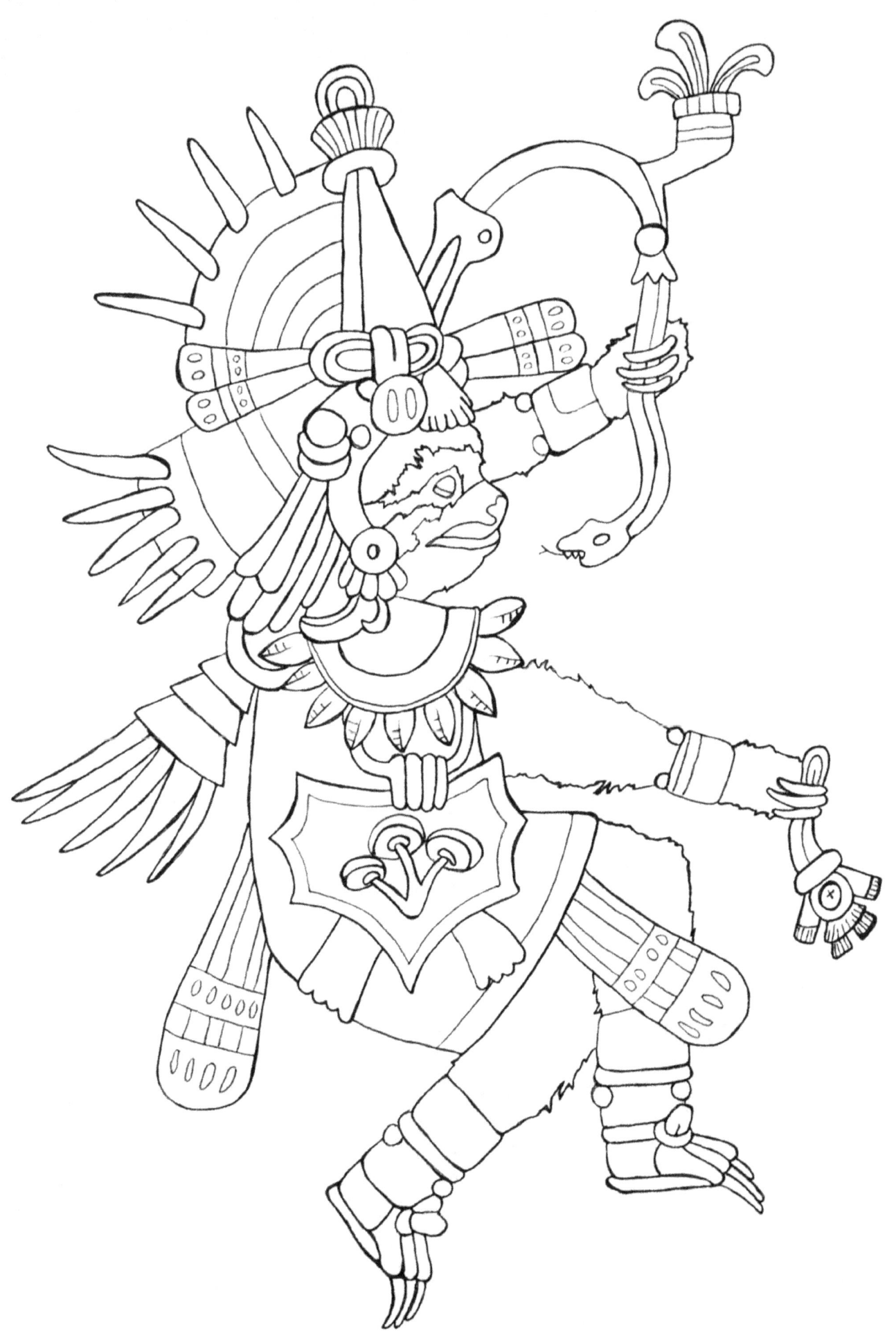

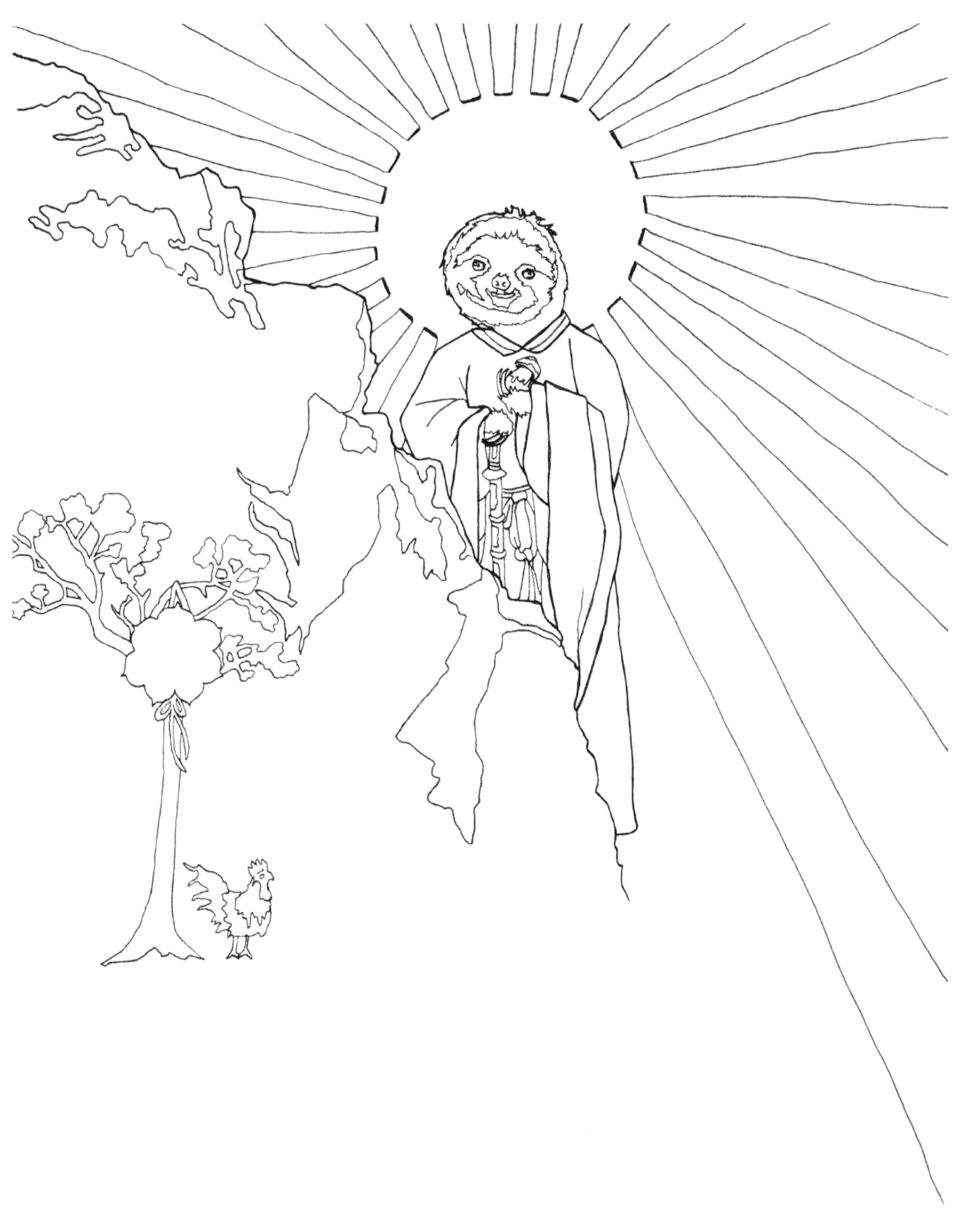

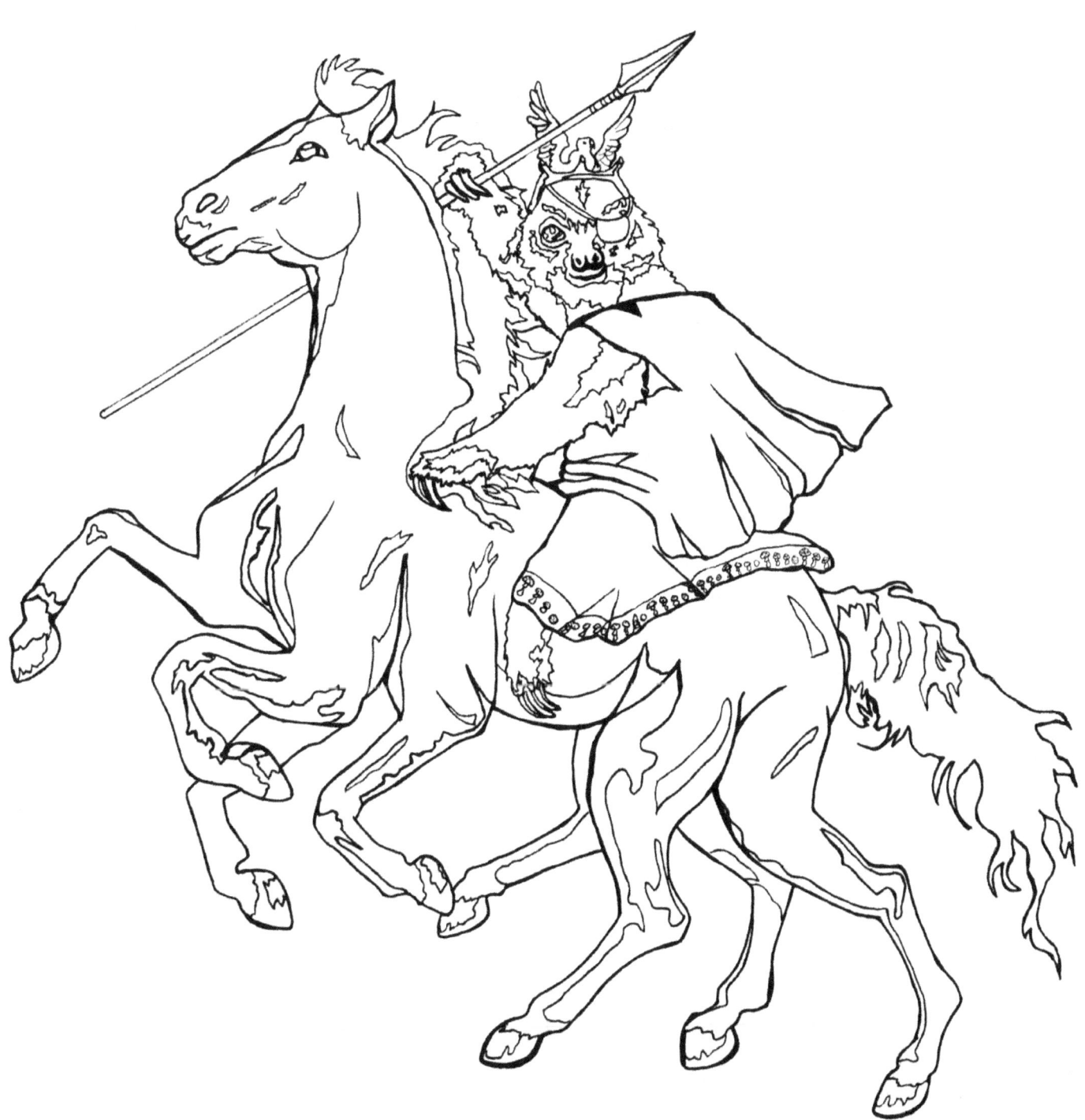

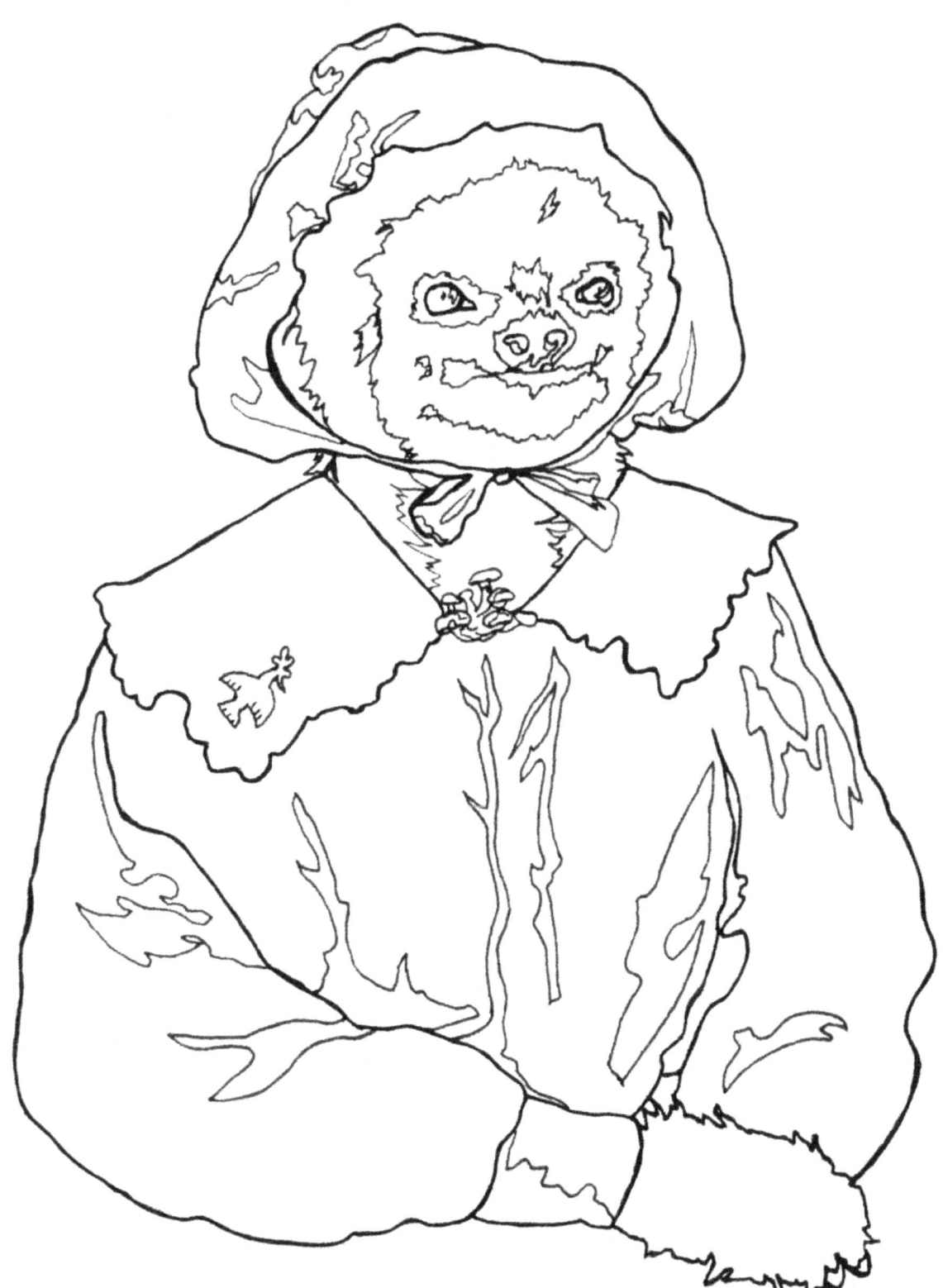

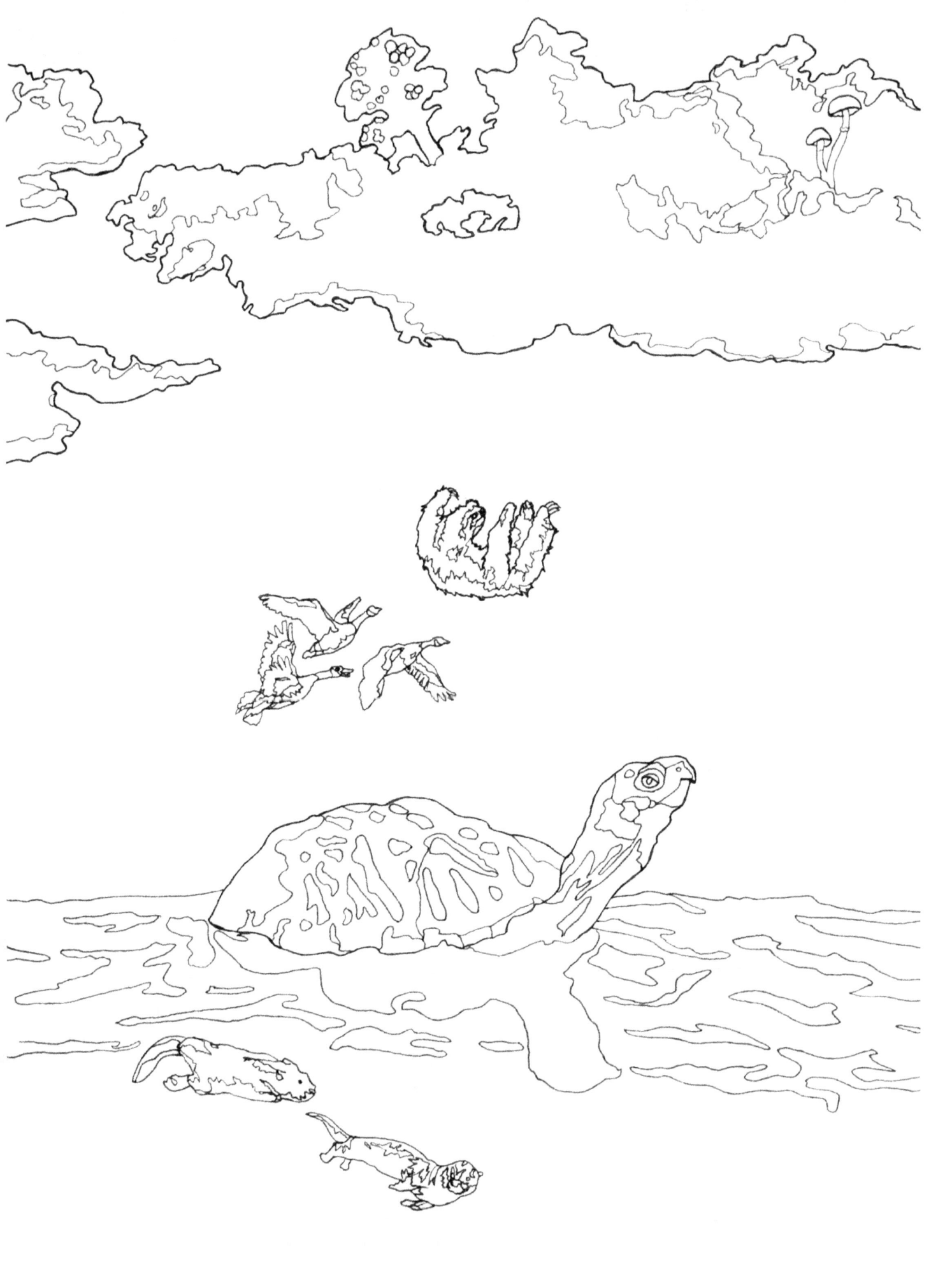

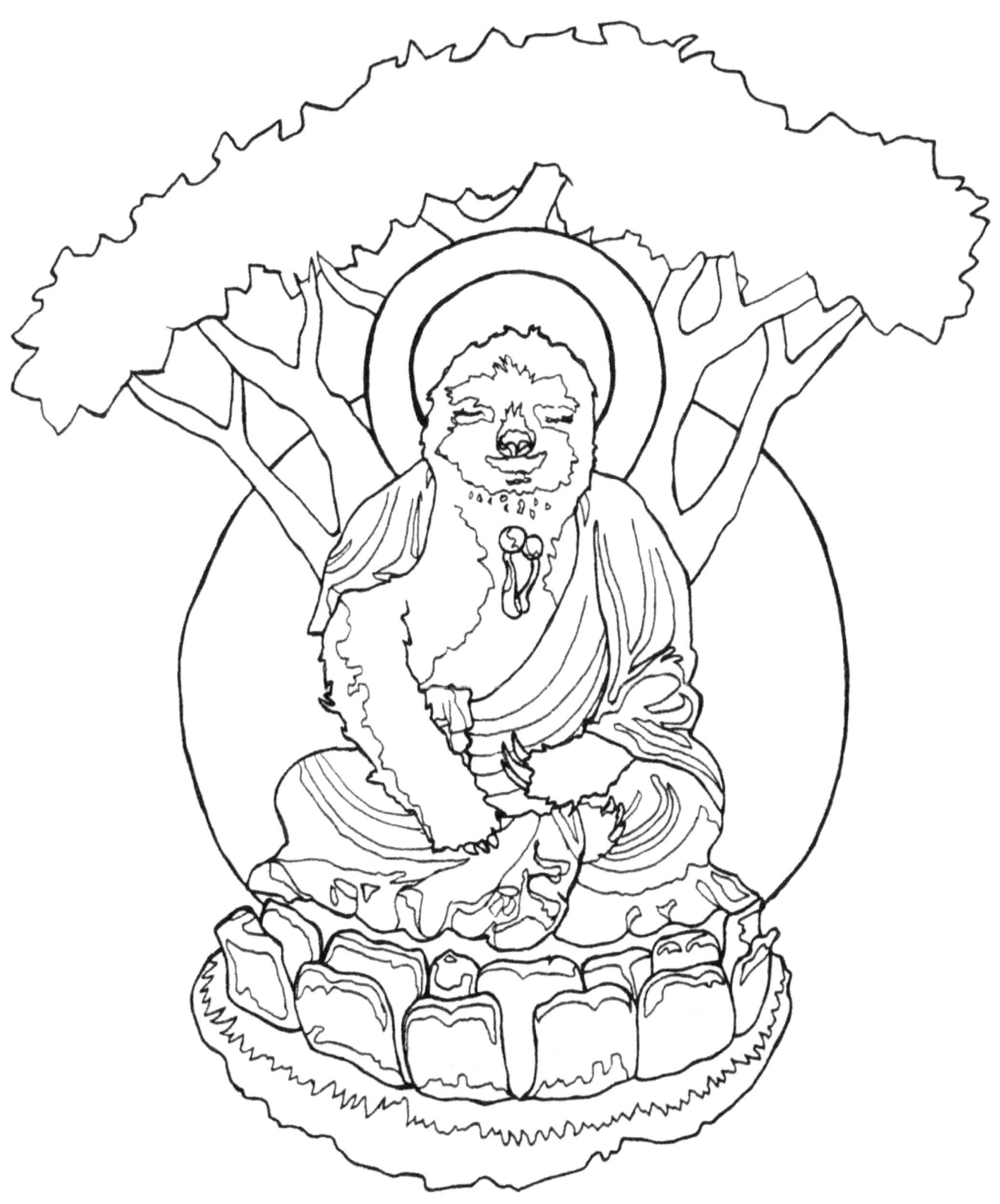

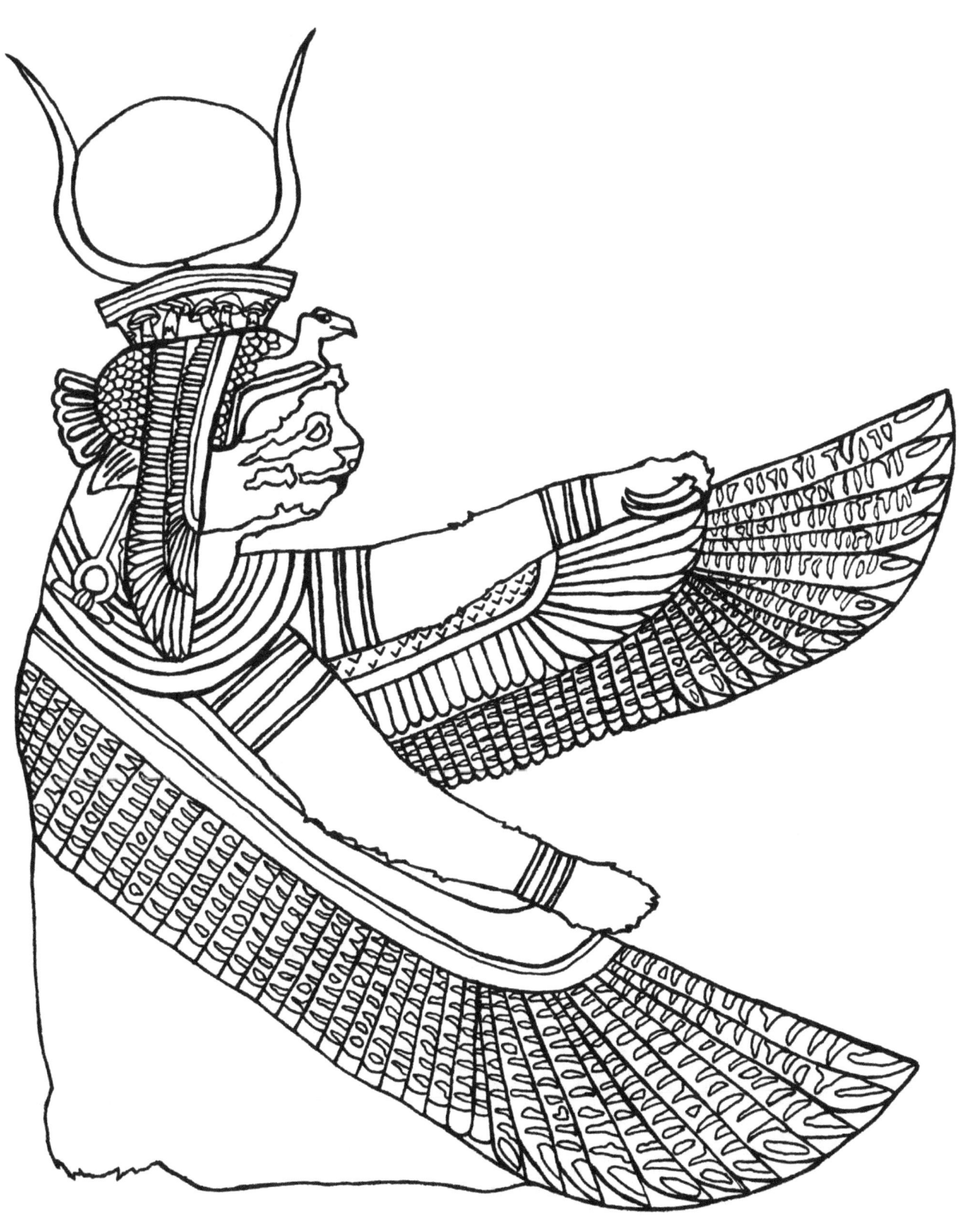

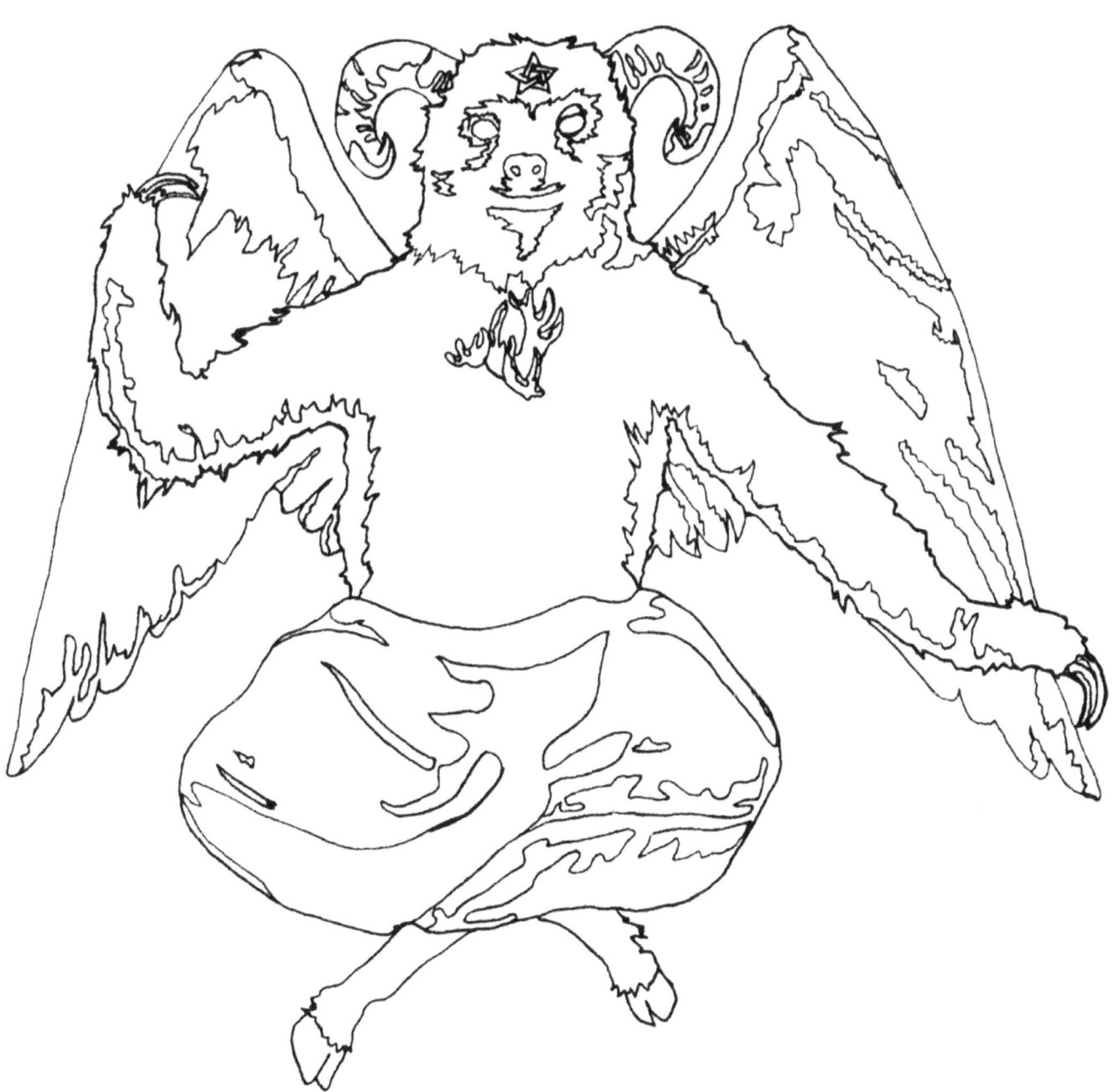

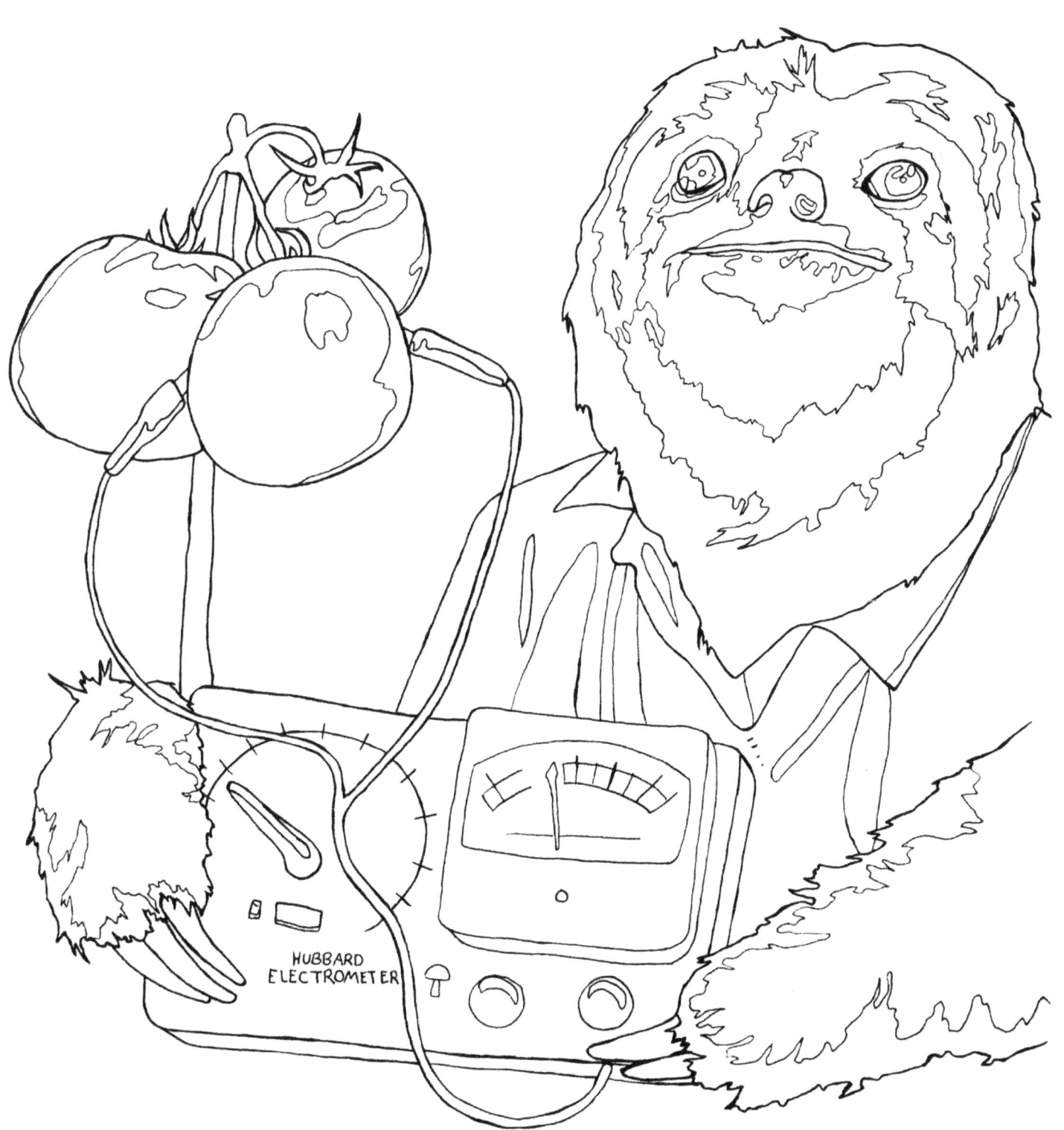

HUBBARD
ELECTROMETER

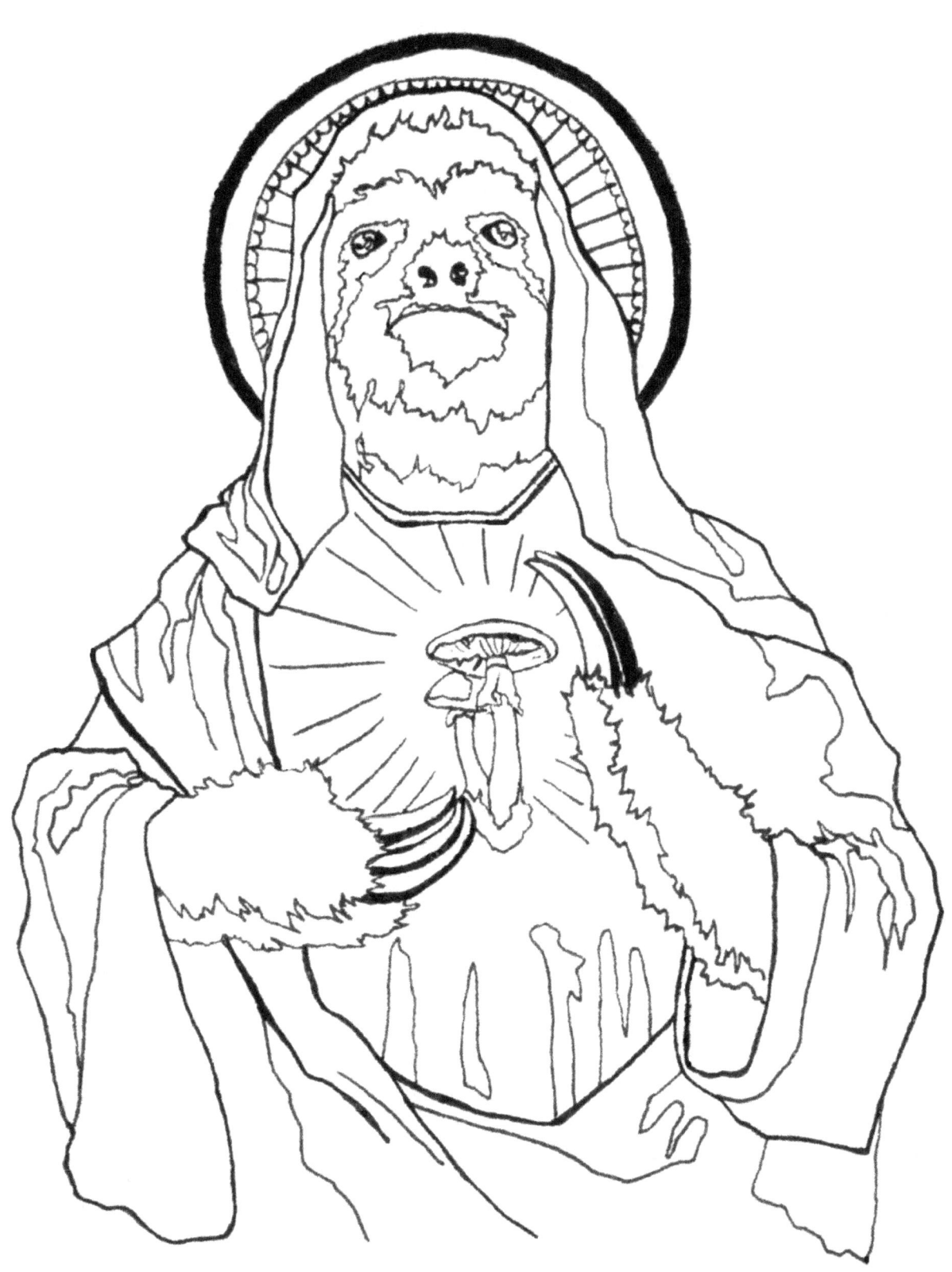

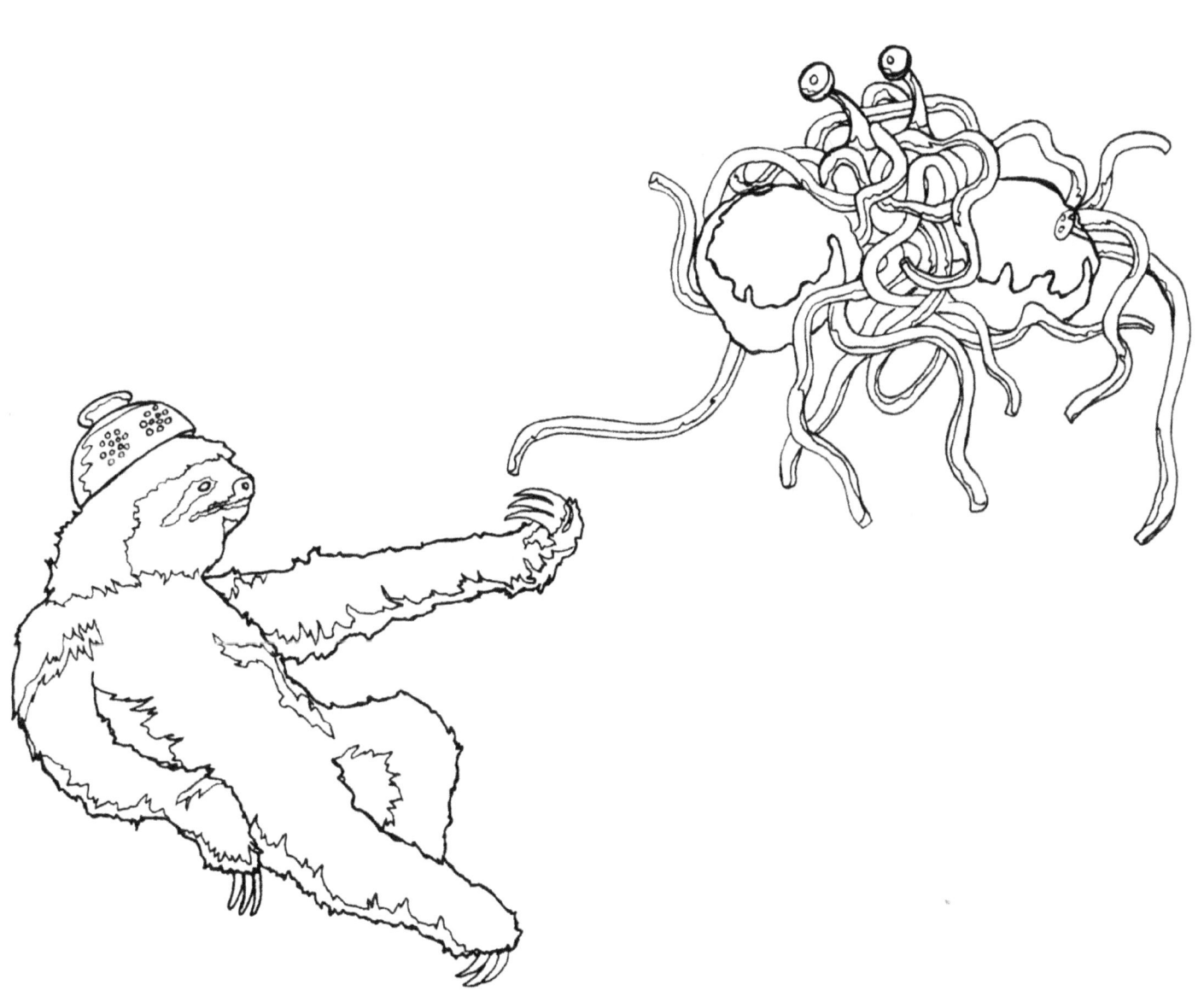

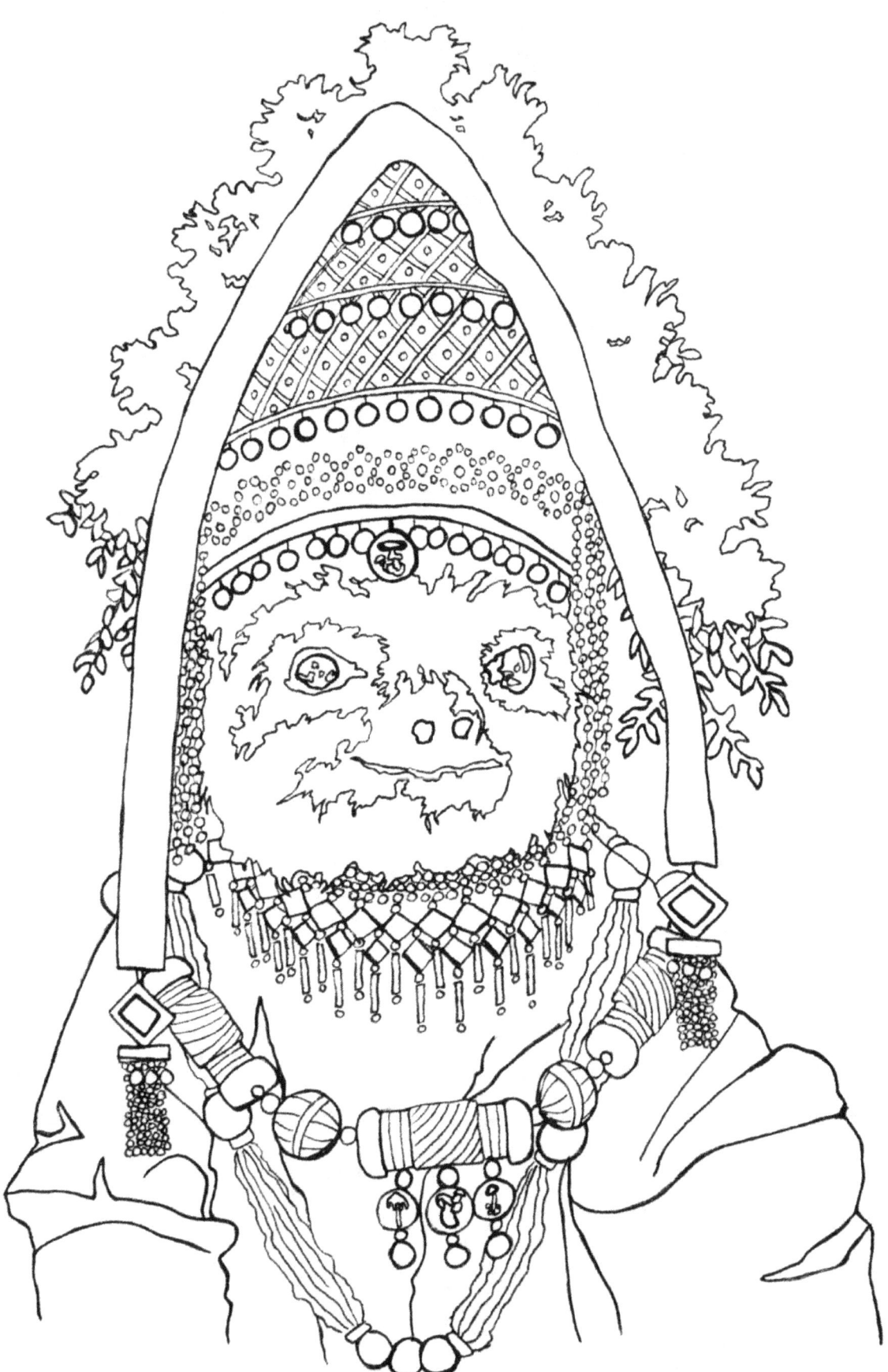

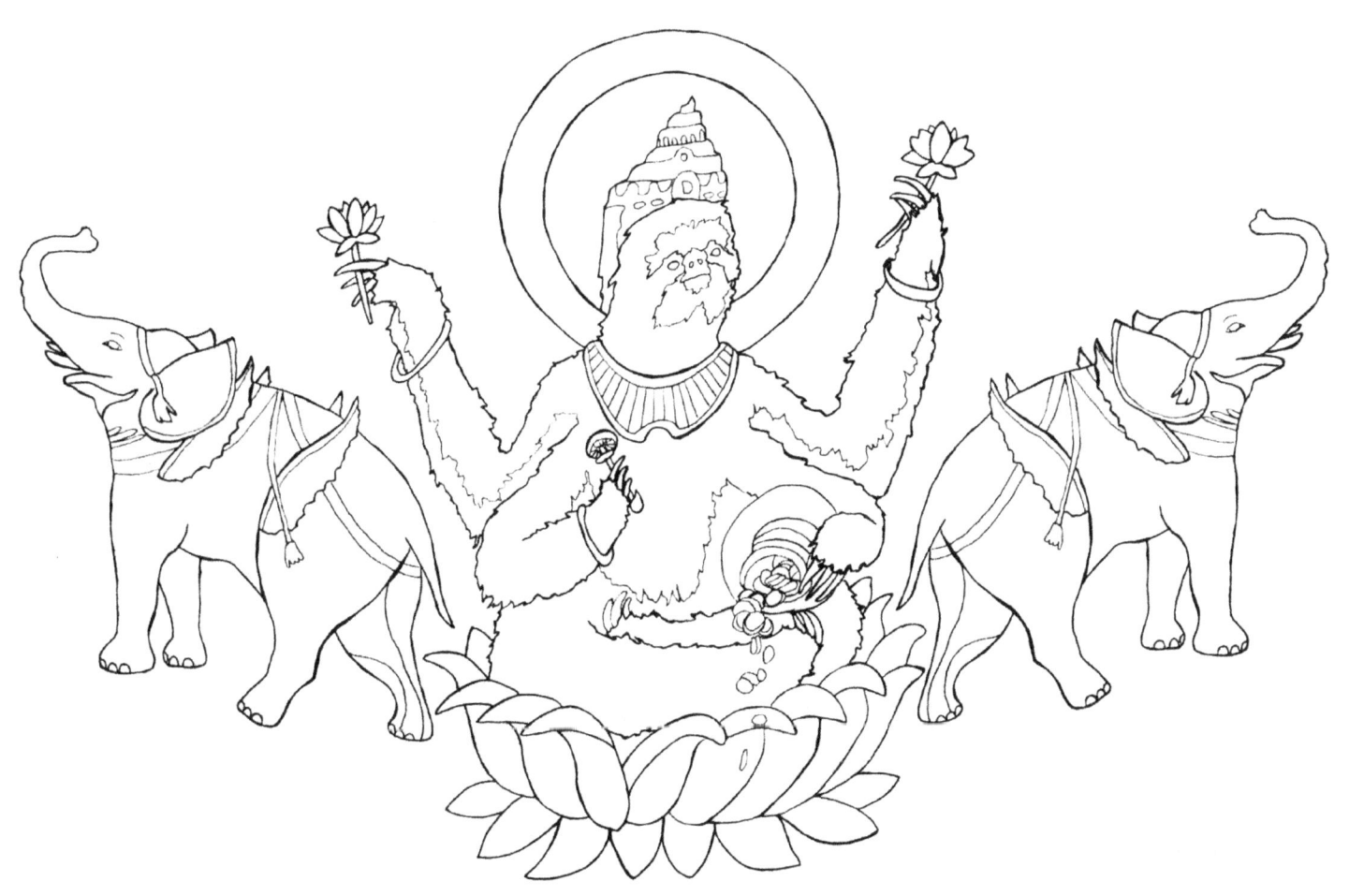

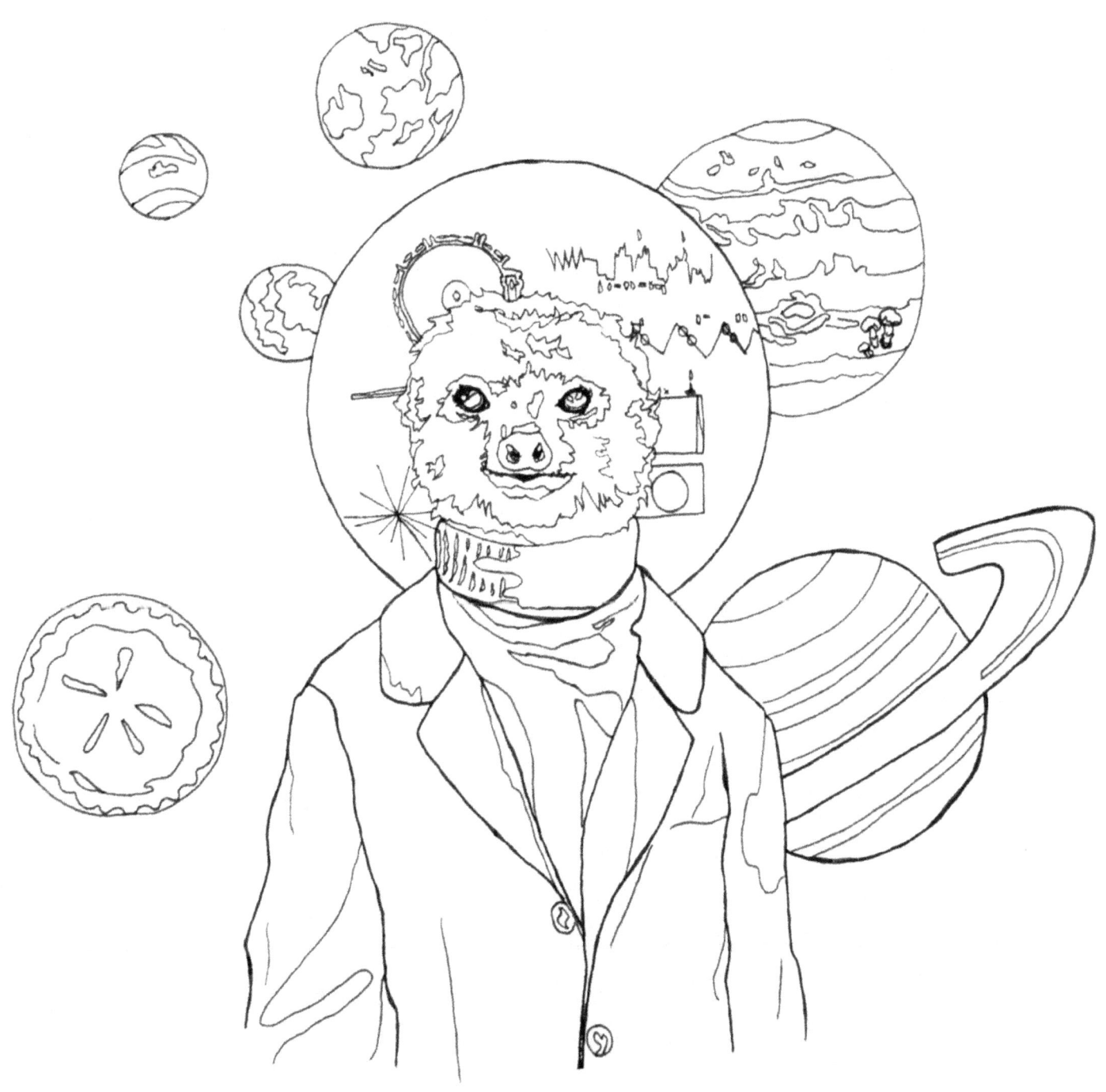

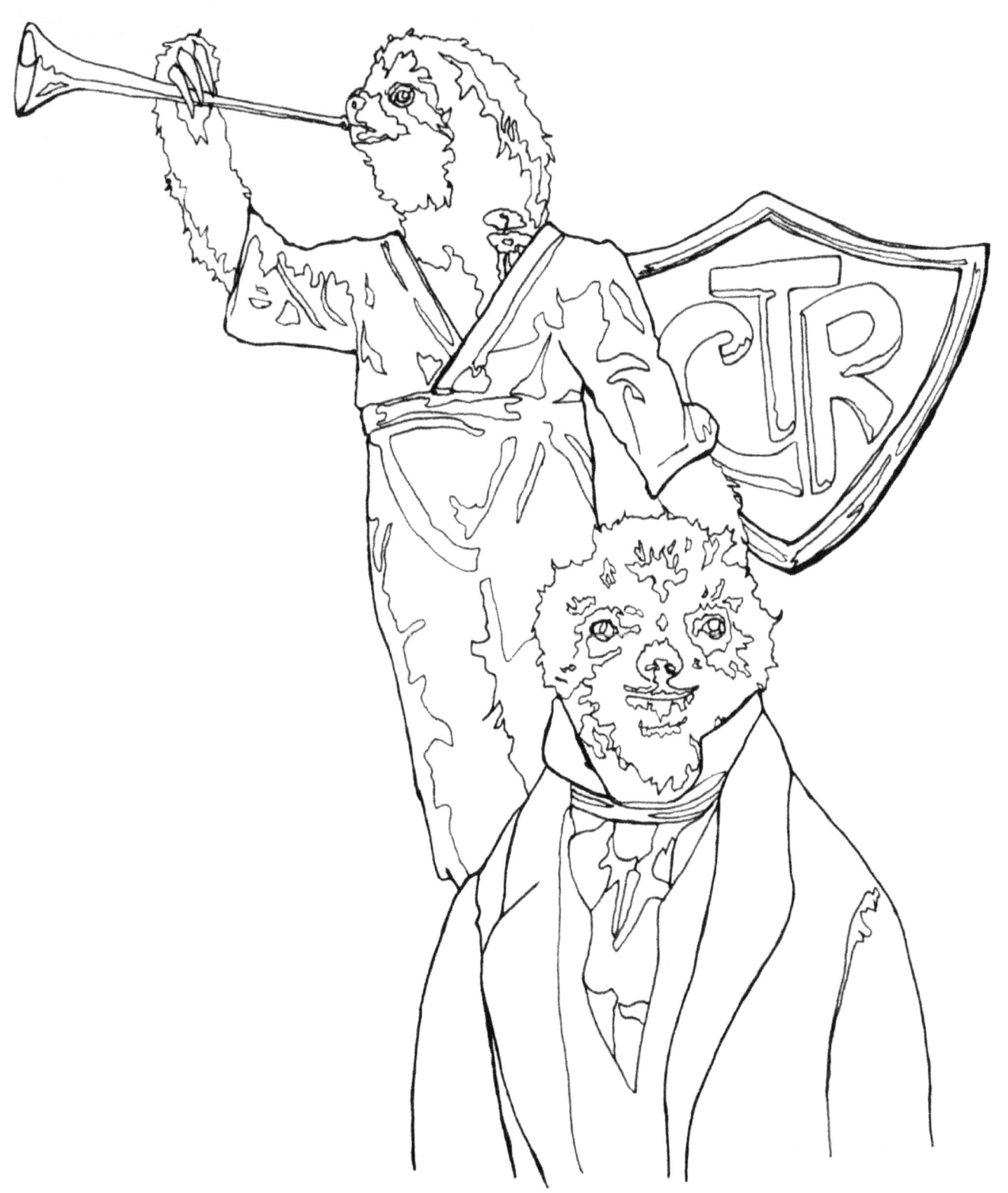

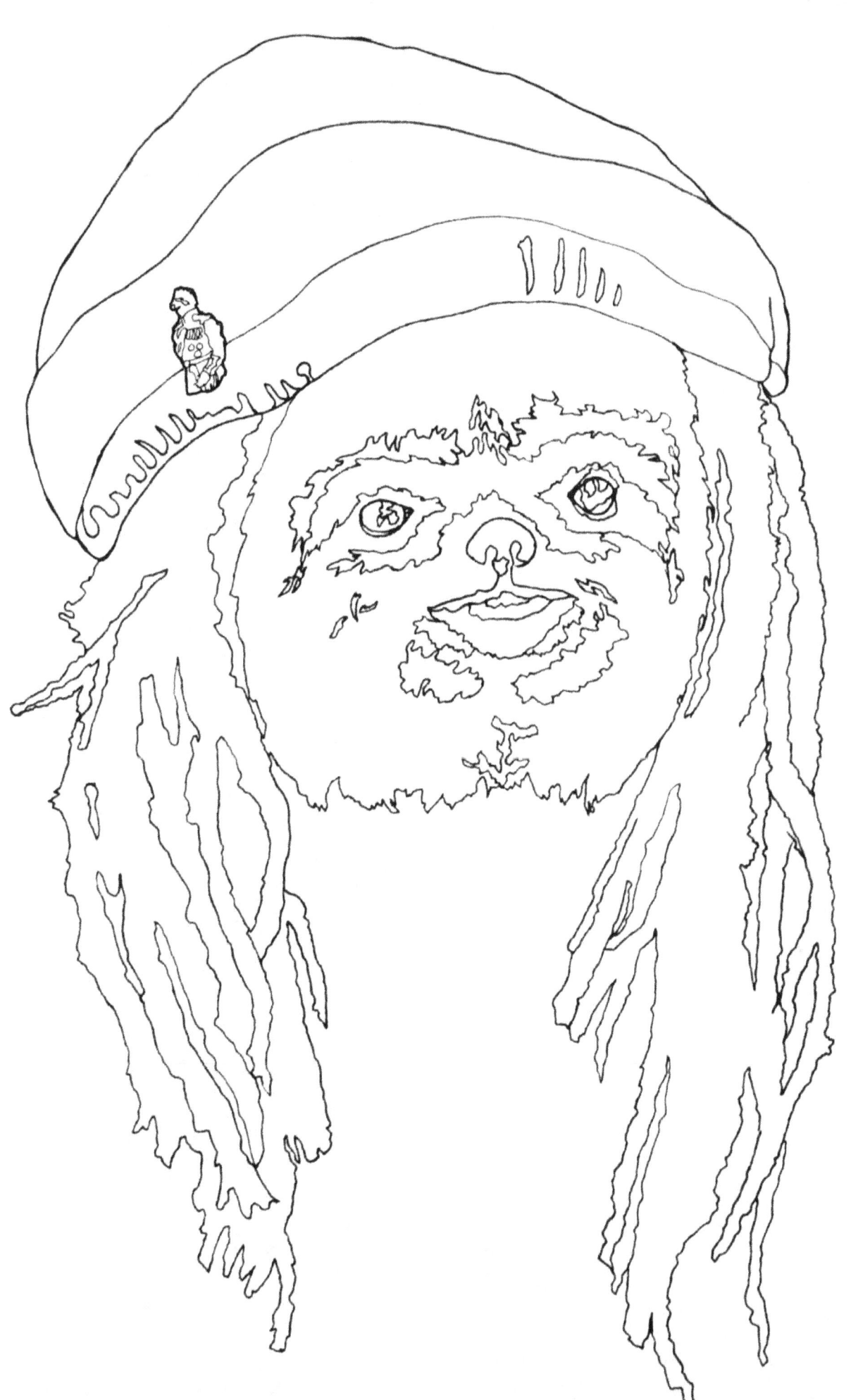

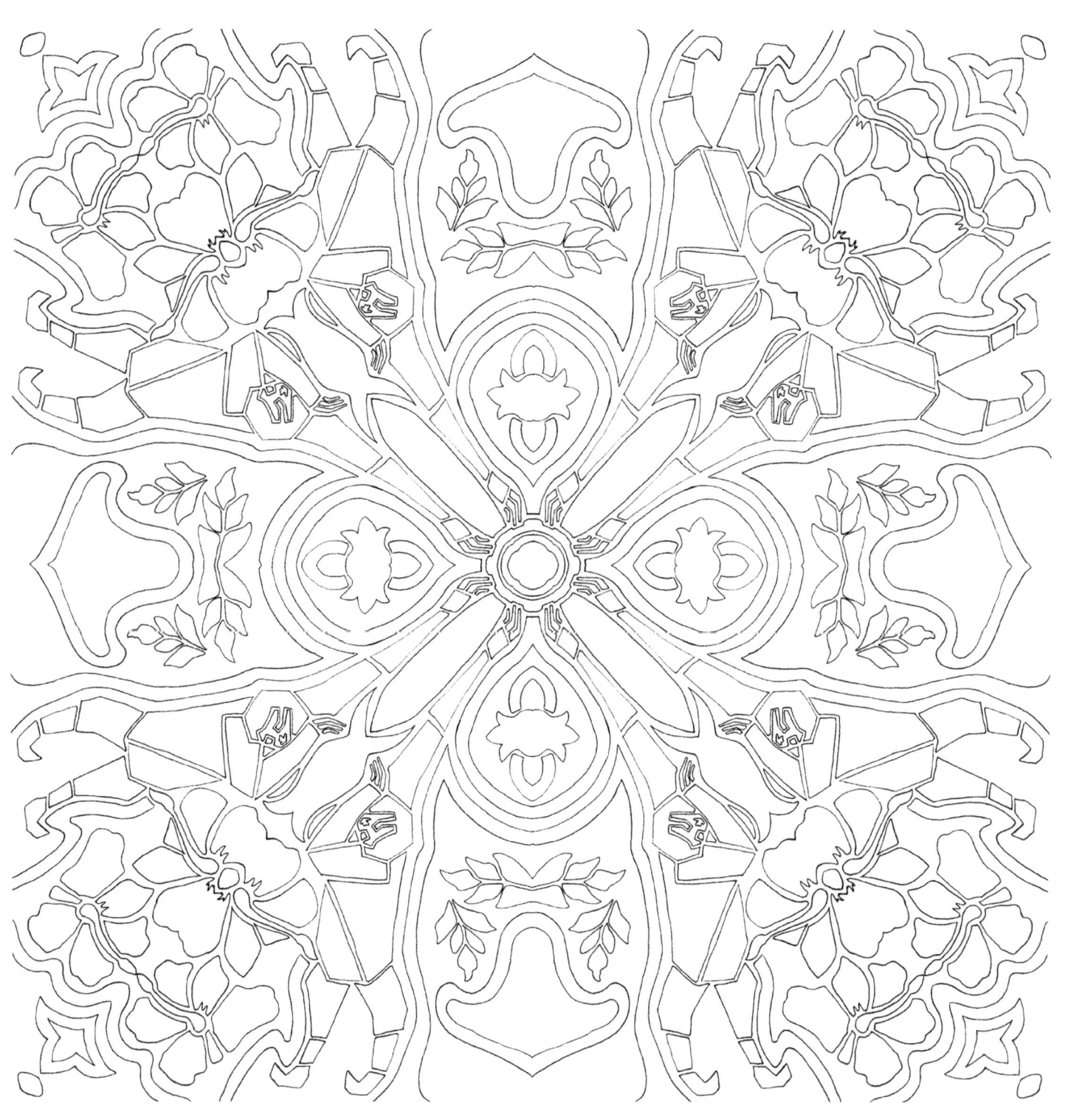

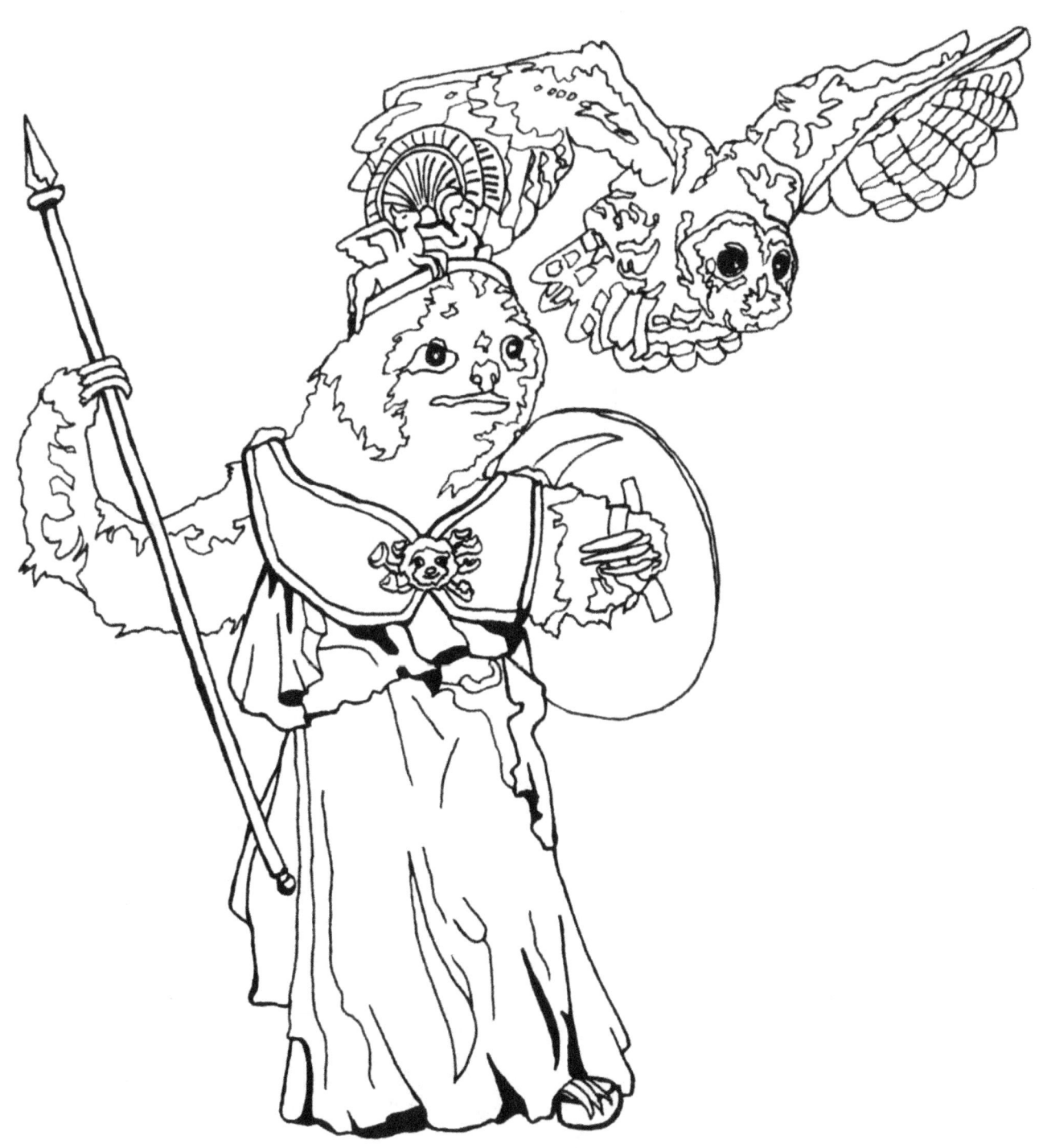

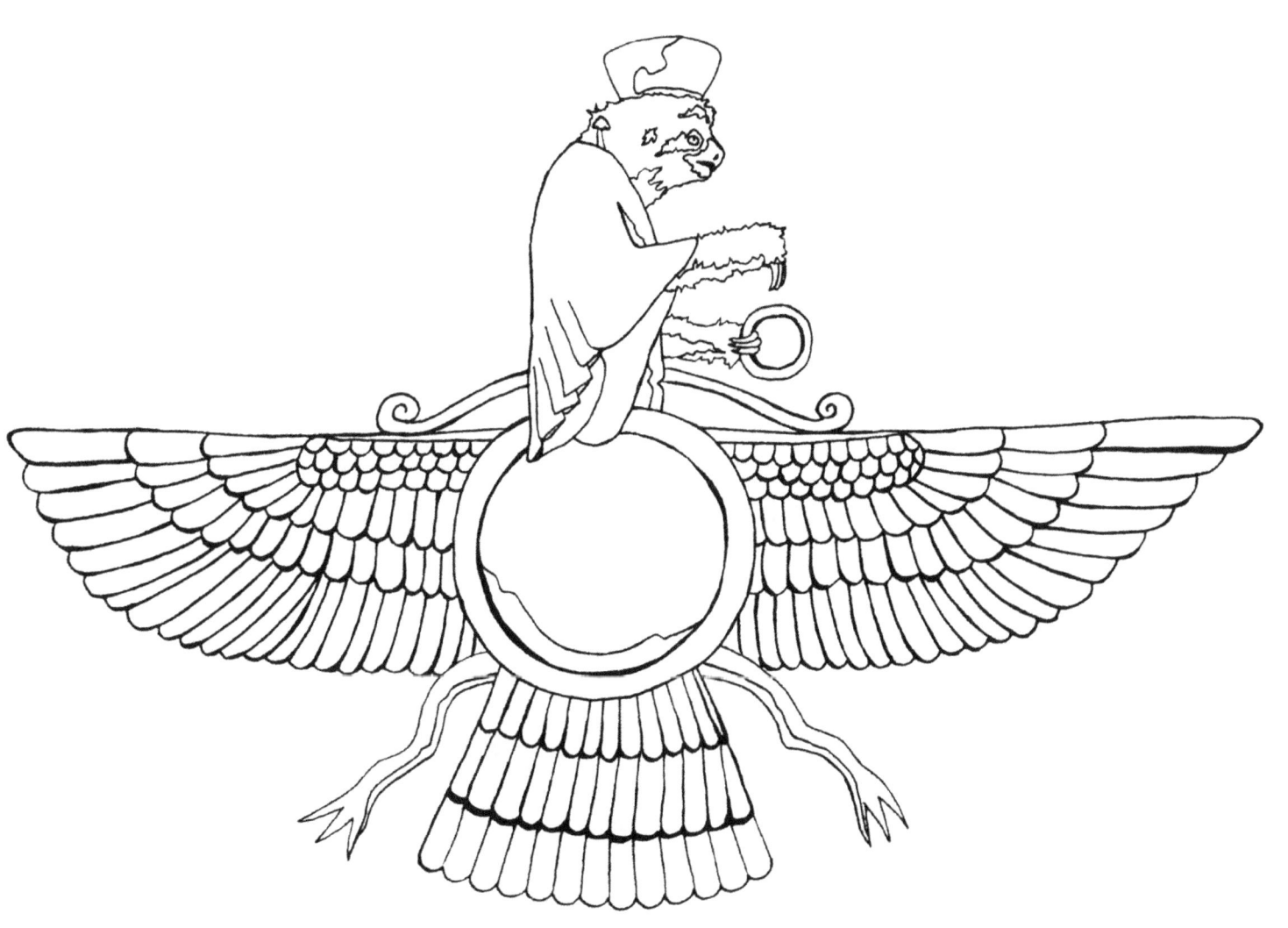

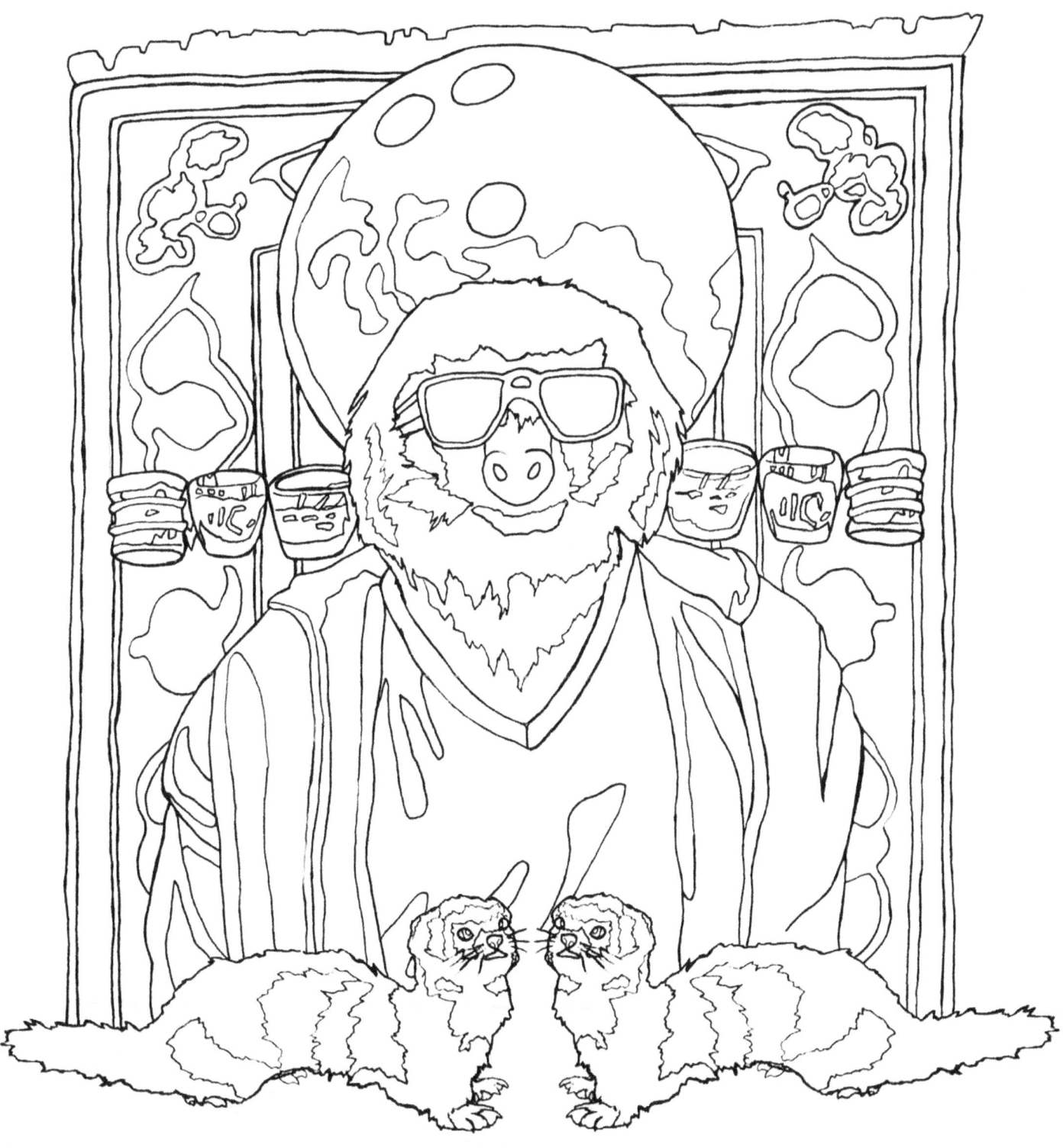

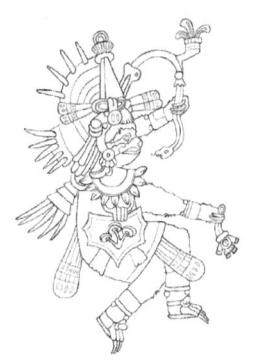

QUETZALCOATL OR
KUKULCAN,
MESO-AMERICAN

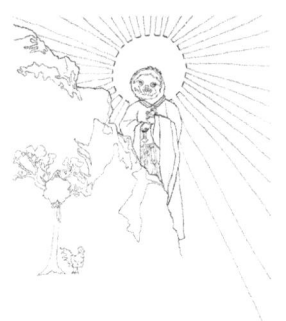

AMATERASU OMIKAMI,
SHINTO

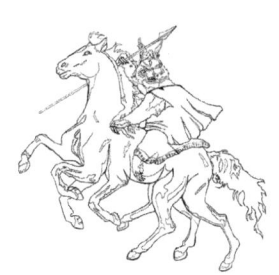

ODIN RIDING SLEIPNIR,
NORSE

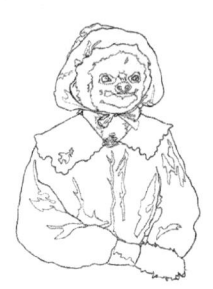

QUAKERISM

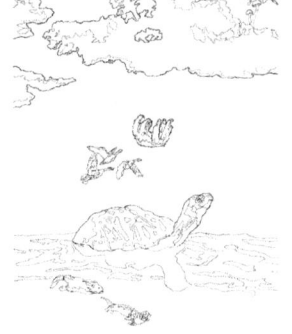

SKY WOMAN,
IROQUOIS CREATION STORY

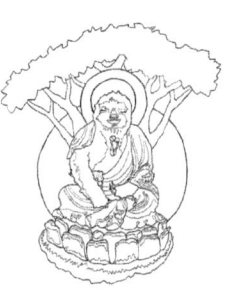

BUDDHISM

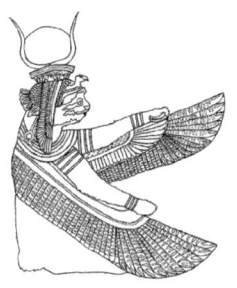

ISIS OR ASET,
ANCIENT EGYPTIAN

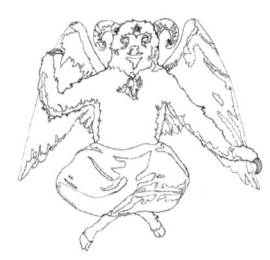

SATANISM

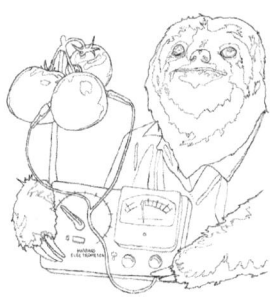

L. RON HUBBARD,
SCIENTOLOGY

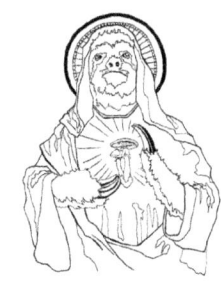

MARY,
CATHOLICISM

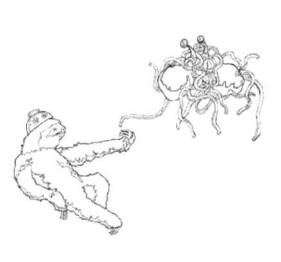

PASTAFARIANISM

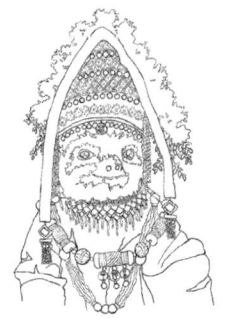

JUDAISM

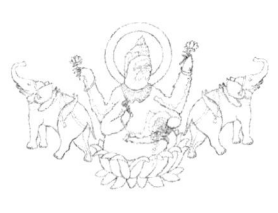

LAKSHMI OR LAXMI,
HINDUISM

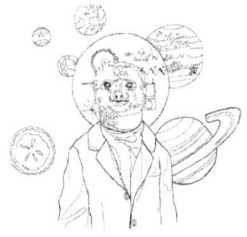

CARL SAGAN,
HUMANISM

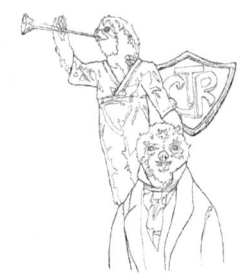

JOSEPH SMITH,
THE CHURCH OF JESUS
CHRIST OF LATTER-DAY
SAINTS

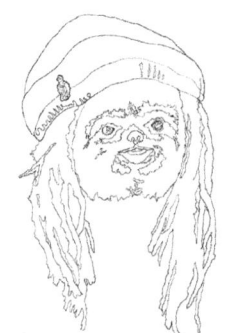

BOB MARLEY,
RASTAFARIANISM

ISLAM

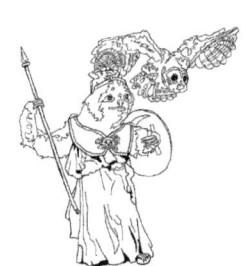

ATHENA OR MINERVA,
POLYTHEISM

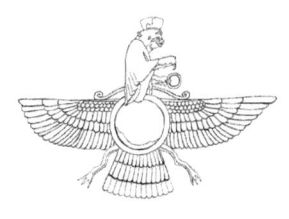

FARAVAHAR OR FEROHAR,
ZOROASTRIANISM

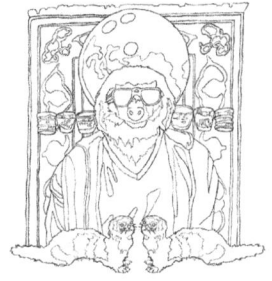

THE DUDE,
DUDEISM

www.ingramcontent.com/pod-product-compliance
Lightning Source LLC
Chambersburg PA
CBHW081133180526
45170CB00008B/3093